We Want The Queen

Overleaf The Queen talking to Londoners on a walkabout on 9 June.

Foreword

I warmly welcome 'We Want the Queen' which Hugo Vickers has compiled for the London Celebrations Committee.

The spontaneous enthusiasm, which far exceeded anyone's wildest expectations, was the Queen's subjects' way of expressing their admiration and gratitude to Her Majesty for her dedication to duty during the past twenty-five years. Excitement reached the summit on Jubilee Day, 7th June, which the Queen declared an extra bank holiday and it was estimated that a crowd of a million, many of whom had waited up all night, turned out to see her. Countless others throughout the world were able to watch the highlights of these events on television, thanks to such organisations as the B.B.C. In U.S.A., the A.B.C. Network was so enthusiastic as to cover live such events as the Silver Jubilee Gala performance at Covent Garden, the Bonfire, and the State Procession and Service at St. Pauls. By a last minute spontaneous decision they added the Firework Night.

The patriotic feeling throughout the country was a visible sign of how the Queen's subjects regard her and the Royal Family. No longer can critics say with any authority that some sections of the community, particularly the younger generation, are apathetic. Despite depressing weather, people were determined to enjoy themselves to a level which has been compared to the Victory Celebrations in 1945. For once national and world problems were forgotten.

Hugo Vickers recaptures many of the 2000 events and 5000 street parties which made 1977 such a memorable year.

PATRICK MONTAGUE-SMITH
EDITOR OF DEBRETT

Acknowledgements

Having worked with the London Celebrations Committee for some months I had a unique opportunity to record the magnificent way in which Londoners celebrated The Queen's Silver Jubilee. With the help of my publisher friend Julian Berry, a full documentary book has become a reality. I am very grateful to Tom Petzal for his assistance throughout and for the benefit of his perambulations through the boroughs.

John Sterling has taken photographs exclusively for this book and became a well-known figure at all Jubilee events. To see him approaching backwards, with camera on high, invariably heralded the start of the show. He was immensely energetic at being in the right place at the right time, but if he didn't feel the right place was good enough he secured a better one to the dumbfoundment of all of us.

For interviews and access to private information, I am most grateful to the Earl of Drogheda, Mr Jeffrey Sterling, Sir Paul Wright, Mr Max Nicholson, Mr Charles Wintour, and Mr John Denison; also to Buckingham Palace Press Office, and to the Home Office. I would like to thank Mr Hugh Montgomery-Massingberd and Miss Diana Keith Neal for their advice. Finally I am deeply indebted to Kate Trevelyan, Chris Green, Anne Dillon, Tessa Feilden, Mary Charteris, Susan Duffus, Amanda Hall and Dana Turner, without whom this book would not have been possible.

Hugo Vickers
London August 1977

Contents

London Celebrations Committee for The Queen's Silver Jubilee

Patrons
HM Lord-Lieutenant of Greater London
The Rt Hon the Lord Mayor of London
The Rt Hon the Chairman of the Greater London Council
The Chairman of the London Boroughs Association

General Committee
The Rt Hon The Earl of Drogheda, KG, KBE, *Chairman*
Jeffrey M. Sterling, CBE, *Deputy Chairman and Honorary Treasurer*

Lt-Col P. R. Adair
John Bosman
Sir Hugh Casson
David Conville
Horace Cutler, OBE
The Rt Rev and Rt Hon Gerald Ellison
Mrs E. Grimsey, MVO
Illtyd Harrington
Sir Michael Hawkins, KCVO, MBE
Councillor L. H. Hilliard, CBE
Rabbi Dr Immanuel Jakobovits
G. J. Kelland, QPM
Neville Labovitch, MBE
Harry G. Lamborn, MP
John Methven
The Rt Hon Lionel Murray, OBE
Geoffrey Peacock
Miss Anne Scott James
Rodney Scrase
Tom Shearer, CB
Sir James Swaffield, CBE
The Rev A. J. Tanner
Alderman A. G. Taylor
Christopher Tugendhat

Sir Paul Wright, KCMG, OBE, *Honorary Secretary General*

The Chairmen of the Programme Committees were also members of the General Committee.

Finance Committee
Jeffrey M. Sterling, CBE, *Chairman*
E. F. Bigland, MBE
Sir Charles Forte
Sir Hugh Fraser, Bt
Nicholas Goodison
Murray Gordon
William Harris
Sir Havelock Hudson
Charles Hughesdon, AFC
Maxwell Joseph
Sir Peter Matthews
Sir Edwin McAlpine
Peter Parker
Francis Perkins, DSC
Sir John Prideaux, OBE
The Lord Rayne
Michael Rivkin
Hon John Sainsbury
Keith Showering
Anthony Tuke
Michael Verey

Media Committee
Charles Wintour, MBE, *Chairman*
John Birt
Peter Black
David Chipp
Jeremy Isaacs
Simon Jenkins
Louis Kirby
Peter Robins
Robin Scott, CBE
Geoffrey Tucker, CBE

Cultural Committee
John Denison, CBE, *Chairman*
Lady Daubeny
Alan Fluck
John Gale
Dr John Hayes
Ian Hunter, MBE
Keith Jeffery
Mrs E. Juda
Sir Robert Mayer, CH
Mrs Edward Sieff
Robert Whyte
Peter Williams
Malcolm Williamson, CBE

Popular Events Committee
The Lord Delfton, *Chairman*
Sir James Carreras, MBE
David Jones, CBE
Eric Morley
Robert Nesbitt
Robert Paterson
Ronald Smart
Brian Tesler

Sports Committee
Jimmy Hill, *Chairman*
Jarvis Astaire
Roger Bottomley
Boris Garside, MC

Environmental Committee
E. M. Nicholson, CB, CVO, *Chairman*
Sir Misha Black, OBE
Neville Labovitch, MBE
Michael Middleton, CBE
Sir Paul Reilly
Robert Shaw

River Events Committee
William Bowey, *Chairman*
E. G. A. Bell, MBE, DSC
Cmdr A. G. F. Crosbie
J. C. Jenkinson
Capt P. A. Leighton
Lt-Cmdr P. F. C. Satow, MBE
G. J. A. Whitehouse, OBE

First published in 1977 by Debrett's Peerage Ltd, 23 Mossop St., London S.W.3.

Paperback ISBN 0 905649 10 9
Hardback ISBN 0 905649 09 5

Produced by the Compton Press Ltd, The Old Brewery, Tisbury, Salisbury, Wiltshire. Designed by Humphrey Stone and Andrew Shoolbred.

Distributed by David Gold & Son (Holdings) Ltd, Units 15–17a Rich Industrial Estate, Crimscott Street, London SE1 5TE.

Printed in Great Britain.

Photographer: John Sterling.

Photo credits: Ashmolean Museum, George Freston of Fox Photos, Mark Gerson, GLC, Kenneth Griffiths, Roger Holmes I.T.C., Kensington and Chelsea Libraries, John Lawrence-Jones, Port of London Authority, Bill Mackenzie, The Press Association, Donald Southern The Times, Madame Tussauds.

Hugo Vickers

We Want The Queen

Debrett's Peerage Limited

Jubilee Beginnings

The origins of Royal Jubilees lie buried in the days of the early Pharaohs some three thousand years before Christ. Thirty years after his accession the Pharaoh had to take part in various ceremonies to demonstrate his continued virility and fitness to rule. One such test was a ritual race he had to run over a prescribed distance. In those days it was called the Heb-sed festival. The word Jubilee is Hebrew and comes from *Yobel*, which refers to the ram's horn with which Jubilee years were proclaimed every 49 years. Medieval Popes also adopted the idea of a Jubilee and this has developed into what the Roman Catholics call Holy Year. Only two early English monarchs marked their Jubilees – Henry III in 1265 and Edward III in 1377, so the first Jubilee to compare with that of 1977 is the Jubilee of King George III in 1809. The economic climate was very bad, and a contemporary historian pointed out 'the Jubilee appears actually to have been a political manoeuvre to divert attention from the incompetence of the Ministry and the shame of the Walchern expedition which had added £20 millions to the National Debt and had covered so many families with mourning'. Jubilee celebrations don't just happen, however, they have to be encouraged and the October 1809 Jubilee was conceived by a body of standing and repute, called the Committee of Merchants and Bankers of the City of London. They provided the spark which caused a spontaneous reaction in the land. Not that everything ran smoothly. There was a fierce dispute over plans for the Lord Mayor of London to give a dinner. One of the supporters of the idea thought he had won, when he claimed the dictionary definition of a Jubilee to be 'a hearty and solemn feast'. This issue and others were fought in the columns of *The Times*, and the dinner only took place after a certain Mr Marriott gave his view that it was 'highly improper to separate with empty stomachs after departing from a cursed cold church'.

It took a letter from Lord Braye to *The Times* on 2 September 1885, which noted that The Queen was 'entering upon her 50th year . . . a year of Jubilee' to inspire the celebrations of 1887. Those of 1897 were

The Queen at the Opening night of the Services Silver Jubilee Musical Pageant 1977 on 30 June.

Opposite The only known mug to anticipate Queen Victoria's Diamond Jubilee, and the longest reign. A circular panel opposite the handle declares 'Longest Reign in English History was attained 23 Septr 1896.'

Opposite below Jubiliana from 1809, with a silhouette of King George III and the inscriptions 'Long Live the King', 'Happy Jubilee', and 'The Father of his People' issued for the King's Jubilee 25 October 1809. Reproduced by gracious permission of Her Majesty The Queen.

anticipated with great eagerness as Queen Victoria at that time held the record of the longest reign since the 72 years of Louis XIV of France. The Silver Jubilee of King George V was first proposed in 1934 and the response was immediate. Only the King himself was diffident about it 'All this fuss and expense about our Jubilee. What will people think of it, these hard and anxious times?'

With these precedents, it is not surprising that for some time before 1977 the Palace and the Home Office were working hard to see that the Silver Jubilee of Queen Elizabeth II did not pass unmarked. At the time of the Queen's Silver Wedding in 1972, an American was so sure of this that he booked a room at the Hilton Hotel then and there so as not to miss any of the fun. Alas the wretched fellow got his dates muddled, thinking the festivities would happen in June 1978 on the twenty-fifth anniversary of the Coronation. Others with a vested interest in any possible celebration were the trades who produce pottery, glass, books and other ephemera to commemorate such occasions. They made a number of direct and indirect approaches to the powers that be and certainly by 1974 were making positive plans. As early as February 1974 King George's Jubilee Trust had conceived the idea of some kind of appeal similar to the one made in 1935. Late in 1974 a Member of Parliament whose hobby was coins, asked a question in the House of Commons on the subject of a new set of coins he hoped might be minted for the Silver Jubilee. He soon found himself the spokesman for the interested parties, and was urged to press for an

Children's Day in Hyde Park on 22 June 1887, part of the celebrations for Queen Victoria's jubilee. A watercolour by R. T. Pritchett, reproduced by gracious permission of Her Majesty The Queen.

announcement about Jubilee plans in general. He wrote several times to the Lord President of the Council and on 27 May 1975 received word from the Home Office that it was too early to say exactly how the occasion was likely to be marked, but that the concern that the arrangements should be announced in good time had been noted.

Nothing further happened until later in 1975. Illtyd Harrington, Deputy Leader of the Greater London Council was the man to play the role of the Lord Braye of ninety years ago. He wrote a letter to the *Evening Standard* which was splashed across the front page on 5 August under the headline 'Let's plan a Royal Jubilee Festival now!'

> The Queen ascended the throne in February 1952. So 1977 will be the year of her Silver Jubilee. What are we going to do about it? A few processions, perhaps; a bit of military pageantry, a thunder of guns in Hyde Park? It would not be enough.

Illtyd Harrington then outlined what he would like to see done. He urged the Government to join in and was confident that private money would soon follow. First, he wanted a focal building to complement the Festival Hall and the National Theatre 'a place where arts can happen, where artists of all kinds can meet the public and where a real feeling of participation in cultural activity can be generated'. This building should also be of use to the commercial world and be adaptable as a fully equipped conference centre. He urged the full use of the three auditoria of the National Theatre, and major seasons of music at Covent Garden, and the Festival Hall and a Ben Jonson/Inigo Jones masque at the Banqueting House. He wanted the museums to mount major exhibitions to celebrate such things as British inventions and the British tradition of adventure and discovery. 'And of course,' he ended, 'don't let us forget the fun, the froth or the splendour. Let's have fireworks, and performances in the parks, and processions on the river. I think Her Majesty will enjoy it just as much as we will ourselves.'

The Palace and the Government had already planned to make their announcements at this time and two days later Roy Jenkins, the Home Secretary, rose to his feet in the House of Commons and made the Silver Jubilee official:

> The Queen has been graciously pleased to approve a recommendation of the Prime Minister that the 25th anniversary of her accession to the throne should be celebrated during the summer of 1977.
>
> The Government are considering how the occasion might most appropriately be marked in compliance with The Queen's express wish that undue expenditure should be avoided. Details of the programme will be announced nearer the time.

The official announcement of a Silver Jubilee combined with Illtyd Harrington's article aroused a strong response in a number of quarters. Harrington received more than two hundred and fifty letters of support. One of them came from Max Nicholson, who had been Secretary of the Lord President of the Council's office from 1945 to 1952 and was an important survivor of Herbert Morrison's Festival of Britain team. 'Your challenging proposals certainly ring a bell with me' he declared. Max Nicholson added that he had further ideas which would lift the festival into 'the realm of inspiration and guidance for the future, which after all was the basis of the Festival of Britain's lasting influence and prestige'.

Charles Wintour, then Editor of the *Evening Standard*, took the initiative. He invited various people to a meeting to discuss a major Royal Jubilee Festival in London, enclosing an outline proposal from Max Nicholson. The meeting took place on 26 September, and shortly afterwards Lord Drogheda agreed to become Chairman of the group, soon to be known as 'The London Celebrations Committee for the Queen's Silver Jubilee'. Lord Drogheda had been connected with both

The Earl of Drogheda, Chairman of the London Celebrations Committee at the Sport for all Spectacular in Hyde Park with Jack Charlton (*left*).

The Financial Times and the Royal Opera House. He invited Jeffrey Sterling to be Treasurer and Deputy-Chairman. Jeffrey Sterling is a young and energetic man from the world of business and finance, with strong cultural interests. They had worked together on the *Britain in Europe* Campaign. Sterling housed the Committee in his office, 4 Carlton Gardens, the wartime Headquarters of General de Gaulle. They forged close links with Buckingham Palace and were given the full backing and support of the Home Office. However, it was made clear that there was no question of any Government cash assisting their work.

The Festival was a good idea, but it was hard to know how to follow it up and bring it to reality. Various plans were in circulation and no one seemed quite clear what the next step should be. The Committee was split up into seven groups – finance, media, sports, cultural, environmental, popular and river events. Jeffrey Sterling chaired the finance committee, and invited onto it leading representatives of as many areas of the commercial world as possible – the top men from the joint stock banks, the insurance companies, Stock Exchange, hoteliers, Accepting Houses Committee and so on.

Charles Wintour chaired the media committee. He invited his counterpart at the Evening News to join him together with senior representa-

Angus Ogilvy taking a glass of celebratory champagne with Jeffrey Sterling, Deputy Chairman and Hon Treasurer of the London Celebrations Committee.

tives from Thames TV, the BBC and London Weekend TV, Capital Radio, BBC Radio London and London Broadcasting, the Editor-in-Chief of the Press Association and others. This Committee was to play a major part in helping to promote Jubilee events throughout the celebrations. Jimmy Hill the football commentator and a leading sports personality, was persuaded to run the Sports Committee. John Denison, who was on the point of retiring as Director of the South Bank Concert Halls, was asked to oversee cultural events. Denison gathered onto his Committee representatives of the Arts Council, the Society of West End Theatre Managers, the Greater London Arts Association, non-agenarian Sir Robert Mayer and others. Max Nicholson was already involved and he took care of environmental matters. He was joined in particular by old Festival of Britain friends, such as Sir Misha Black (who died in August 1977), and Sir Hugh Casson. Sir Bernard (later Lord) Delfont was a natural for popular events and had the advantage of heading a self financing operation. William Bowey, Managing Director of the Port of London Authority, headed the River Events Committee and appointed Tony Bell as their secretary.

Every effort was made to ensure that the Committee represented London as a whole. The Patrons were the Lord-Lieutenant, the Lord Mayor, the Chairman of the GLC, and the Chairman of the London Boroughs Association. Furthermore the Committee included a Conservative and Labour MP, and representatives from the Police, the Ministry of Defence, the TUC, the Department of the Environment, the Churches and the Civil Service. In those early days and throughout, the Committee leaned heavily on the enthusiasm and experience of the GLC's Director General, Sir James Swaffield.

Clearly it was important to find an honorary Secretary-General to co-ordinate activities and run a small secretariat. Sir Paul Wright was the retired Ambassador to the Lebanon and still had special duties on behalf of the Foreign Secretary. These duties included welcoming visiting dignitaries at Heathrow Airport and had earned him the endearing sobriquet of 'The Smiler' in royal circles. By coincidence Sir Paul had also been involved in the Festival of Britain as Director of Public Relations. In contrast to the august committee, the secretariat comprised a small group of enthusiasts, all in their early thirties or younger.

On 29 January 1976 the establishment of the Committee was welcomed by the Home Secretary in the House of Commons, and backed a few weeks later by a statement from Margaret Thatcher. Jeffrey Sterling was now ready to raise funds, an operation which lasted from March to May 1976. Nobody needed to be convinced as to why the Queen's Jubilee should be celebrated, but they did want to know how the money would be spent. Amounts poured in from £25,000 to £100. Michael Verey, Chairman of the Accepting Houses Committee, was twenty-two at the time of King George V's Jubilee. He remembered walking arm-in-arm with the crowds in the Mall in 1935. At that time

Opposite Jimmy Hill riding a bicycle in St James's Park at the start of the Jubilee Veteran Cycle Race, a sponsored 1,000 mile ride for veterans from London to Balmoral and back, which took place between 5 and 14 June.

the Government had voted a small sum for the Jubilee Celebrations, and rather shamefacedly voted more when they realised its potential. Michael Verey spoke for many when he said that it was not right for the Government to pay for the festivities, we should do it ourselves. He backed his words with a substantial cheque from his firm.

The London Celebrations only just got their plea for funds in before King George's Jubilee Trust announced the Queen's Silver Jubilee Appeal. The Appeal wanted money for youth projects, and the London Celebrations Committee wanted money to ensure that the Jubilee was worthily celebrated, two quite different things, but both wanted donations. Confusion between the two organisations lasted throughout the year and even the Prince of Wales found that people were always asking him to take part in Jubilee occasions, thinking he was running the whole Jubilee whereas he was only in charge of the Appeal. Eventually the London Celebrations Committee raised a sum in excess of £500,000, though further substantial sums were donated to special projects.

The Queen's Diary

The 6 February 1977, the twenty-fifth anniversary of the death of King George VI and accession of Queen Elizabeth II fell by chance on a Sunday. It was appropriate that the day should be spent quietly at Windsor. The Queen and the Duke of Edinburgh, the Prince of Wales, Queen Elizabeth the Queen Mother, Princess Anne, Prince Edward and Princess Margaret attended morning service in the Royal Chapel in Windsor Great Park, as they always do when they are at Windsor for the weekend. The service was private to the Royal Family and those who live on the estate and only a handful of members of the public gathered at the entrance of Royal Lodge to see the Queen arrive. The Chapel was decorated with azaleas and Spring flowers and the service included a special accession day prayer.

The Sunday papers did not neglect the occasion, and all looked back over the first twenty-five years of the Queen's reign. *The Sunday Times* concentrated on the constitutional role of the Sovereign and examined the occasions on which the Queen had been drawn into the political arena. It concluded: 'The Queen personally has very few critics. The monarchy as an institution has some. That is inevitable, because monarchy is not a world-wide fashion. Yet such criticisms count for little against the benefits that the Queen confers.' *The Sunday Telegraph* noted that whereas Great Britain had experienced national decline since 1952, the Queen's own reputation and the institution she embodies, had gone from strength to strength. *The Observer* pointed out that the Queen had tried to democratise the monarchical role by extending the range of the Royal Family's personal contacts and public activities. 'In this way, the monarchy has become largely de-mythologised . . . without losing the glamour and mystique of State occasions.' It spoke of the Royal Family as 'conscientious and tireless workers' and ended 'The Queen has fulfilled her role with a brilliance that carefully conceals itself behind the conventions. Long may she reign.' Nor was the Duke of Edinburgh to remain silent on the great day. In an article in the *Sunday Mirror* he plunged into an erudite survey not only of the

Opposite The Queen and the Duke of Edinburgh followed by the Queen Mother, Prince Edward, Princess Anne and Princess Margaret leaving Royal Lodge Chapel after morning service on 6 February.

Queen's reign but of how the innovations of the Industrial Revolution were only just coming home to roost. Sir John Betjeman's Jubilee hymn was published and caused instant controversy, and collectors of royal photographs were confronted by glorious colour pictures of the Queen, her family, her hats and her regalia, with which to fill their scrapbooks.

Because it was a Sunday, the traditional royal salutes were delayed until Monday. As protocol demands, a forty-one gun salute was fired at noon in Hyde Park by the King's Troop of the Royal Horse Artillery,

A Royal Salute being fired at the Tower of London.

The Queen undertaking her first jubilee engagement in London when she planted a Lucombe Oak in Victoria Tower Gardens on 8 February.

and a sixty-two gun salute was fired an hour later at the Tower of London by the men of the Honourable Artillery Company.

The Queen was scheduled to leave London on Wednesday, 9 February for her first overseas Jubilee tour, which included visits to Australia and New Zealand, but she made a London Jubilee appearance in the Victoria Tower Gardens at 3 pm. on Tuesday, 8 February. Accompanied by the Duke of Edinburgh, the Queen formally planted a Lucombe Oak Tree, a tree that was the first of many to be planted throughout the Greater London Area under the auspices of the London Tree Group, a sub-committee of the London Celebrations Committee. Because several million trees had been lost in the United Kingdom during the past twenty-five years for a variety of reasons, the London Tree Group was established to encourage the planting of new trees not only to mark the Jubilee, but to bring long-term benefit to different London environments. On 20 April the Queen made a visit to Hyde Park to plant a silver birch tree at a point in the park opposite the Dorchester Hotel in Park Lane.

Many of the leader writers on 6 February asked what part the Queen would play in the reshaping of the United Kingdom in the event of devolution. On Wednesday, 4 May the Queen gave them a clue as to how she felt on that particularly topical problem. The 4 May marked the official beginning of the Silver Jubilee celebrations in the United Kingdom and was the first occasion in the year when crowds gathered in the streets of London. The Queen and the Duke of Edinburgh went to Westminster to receive the loyal addresses of both Houses of Parliament. The previous day the Prime Minister had moved that the Address should be presented to the Queen. Speaking in the House of Commons, he spoke of the Throne as the summit of the country and a unifying influence for the people. However, he made it clear that the Speaker's address was to be presented to the Queen as a person and not to the Throne as an institution. He was supported by Margaret Thatcher and David Steel and the motion was formally agreed to. So too was a similar motion in the House of Lords.

The ceremony took place in Westminster Hall and was one of those few occasions when the three vital elements of the constitution, Sovereign, Lords (spiritual and temporal) and Commons meet under one roof. Also present were judges, members of the diplomatic corps and a few distinguished guests such as Harold Macmillan. The Queen Mother, the Prince of Wales, Princess Anne, Captain Mark Phillips and Princess Margaret arrived at 11.55 am., and to a fanfare of trumpets and the covering of the maces in the royal presence, the Queen and the Duke entered the Hall from St. Stephen's Entrance. The Lord Chancellor, Lord Elwyn-Jones, read and presented the first address, and the Speaker of the House of Commons, the Rt. Hon. George Thomas followed. The Queen then replied and included in her speech her now famous, controversial reference to the problems of devolution:

The Sovereign (*centre*) the Lords (*left*) and the Commons (*right*) gathered in Westminster Hall for the presentation of loyal addresses on 4 May.

I number Kings and Queens of England and of Scotland, and Princes of Wales among my ancestors and so I can readily understand these aspirations. But I cannot forget that I was crowned Queen of the United Kingdom of Great Britain and Northern Ireland. Perhaps this Jubilee is a time to remind ourselves of the benefits which union has conferred, at home and in our international dealings, on the inhabitants of all parts of this United Kingdom.

On 6 May the Queen visited the Peel Centre, the Metropolitan Police's training establishment at Hendon. There was a garden party and an exhibition demonstrating the changes in police techniques during the reign. The Queen was presented with a silver model of a policeman in 1952 uniform and inspected a guard of honour commanded by Mr Frederick Drayton Porter, now Chief Constable of Cambridgeshire, who has the distinction of being the only present serving officer in the force to have attended a Silver Jubilee Police Review by King George V in 1935. On Saturday, 7 May the Queen reviewed a Parade of vintage Rolls-Royces at Windsor and that evening entertained President Carter and six other world leaders to dinner at Buckingham Palace after their economic summit at Number Ten Downing Street. A further dinner for NATO foreign ministers was held on Tuesday, 10 May. The Queen then left London to tour Scotland until 27 May.

The Queen travelled to Windsor from Edinburgh and on Saturday, 28 May attended the Royal Windsor Big Top Show in the Home Park. This performance, later seen on television, included a David Frost interview with Mike Yarwood's impersonation of the Prince of Wales.

It is traditional to celebrate State occasions with a Gala at Covent Garden. For example, a Gala was held during the State Visit of President Giscard d'Estaing of France in June, 1976. The Gala Performance of Opera and Ballet held at the Royal Opera House on Monday, 30 May, was a magnificent occasion. Sixteen members of the Royal Family attended, headed by the Queen and the Duke of Edinburgh and were greeted by the joint hosts, the Earl of Drogheda, Chairman of the London Celebrations Committee and no stranger to Covent Garden, and Sir Claus Moser, Chairman of The Royal Opera House. The invitations stipulated 'Evening dress and decorations' and the entrance foyer was filled with distinguished guests in white ties and sashes of orders, and ladies in their finest evening gowns and tiaras. The Yeomen of the Guard, added a splash of scarlet as they lined the staircase. The scene whispered the lost enchantments of Vienna at the turn of the century.

In the Royal Box the Queen, the Duke of Edinburgh, the Queen Mother, and the Prince of Wales wore the magnificent blue riband of the Most Noble Order of the Garter from the left shoulder. There were two unique orders in the Royal Box that night. Princess Alice, Duchess of Gloucester is the first and only Dame Grand Cross of the Order of the

The Queen and the Duke of Edinburgh entertaining President Jimmy Carter at Buckingham Palace on 7 May.

Left The Queen and the Duke of Edinburgh with (behind) Sir Claus Moser.

Above The Earl and Countess of Drogheda greeting the Duke and Duchess of Kent at the Royal Opera House, Covent Garden on 30 May.

Below Princess Alice, Duchess of Gloucester wearing the riband of the Order of the Bath and Princess Alice, Countess of Athlone with Sir Claus and Lady Moser and Mr and Mrs John Tooley.

Left The Prince of Wales, Princess Anne and Captain Mark Phillips at the Royal Opera House.
Above Princess Margaret, Countess of Snowdon. In the background are the Earl and Countess of Drogheda.
Below The Queen and the Duke of Edinburgh back stage after the performance with Sir Frederick Ashton.

Left The Queen and members of the Royal Family in the Royal Box at the Silver Jubilee Gala.

Above The Queen backstage after the Silver Jubilee Gala. Kenneth Macmillan, then Director of the Royal Ballet, with the presentation line (left to right) Ann Jenner, David Wall, Merle Park, Rudolf Nureyev and Margot Fonteyn.

Bath and she wore its red riband, and 94-year-old Princess Alice, Countess of Athlone, the last surviving granddaughter of Queen Victoria wore the Order of Victoria and Albert given to her by her grandmother in 1898.

The programme began with a fanfare from the Trumpeters of the Royal Military School of Music at Kneller Hall, followed by the National Anthem. 'Hail, all Hail to the Queen,' an extract from Berlioz's *The Trojans*, with magnificent Trojans marching down both aisles and onto the stage, introduced the operatic part of the programme. Extracts from Rossini, Verdi, Mozart, Donizetti and Beethoven followed. The second half was dedicated to ballet and included the choral dances from Britten's *Gloriana*, and Frederick Ashton's *Hamlet Prelude*, a *pas de deux* to music by Liszt, which was danced by Rudolf Nureyev and Margot Fonteyn. Prudence Glynn, fashion editor of *The Times*, noted that the Prime Minister was the only man visibly intoning the National Anthem at the beginning of the performance but that at the reprise which ended the programme 'the mouths of most of the audience were loyally agape'. The National Anthem over, hundreds of tiny silver discs were released from the dome of the Opera House and fluttered amongst the audience like confetti. The Royal Family then went backstage to meet members of the cast and the orchestra. The entire programme was shown live on television, not only at home but all over the world.

A week later, on 6 June, the Queen drove from Windsor Castle by torchlight procession to Snow Hill to light the Royal Beacon, the first of 102 beacons across the country to announce that the Silver Jubilee festivities had begun. This act was a landmark in the Queen's reign and had a fitting historic precedent. Queen Elizabeth I had bonfires lit to warn her people of the approaching Spanish Armada in 1588. Indeed, when Sir Martin Charteris, the Queen's Private Secretary, was discussing plans for Windsor's festivities two years previously, he had quoted Macaulay:

> At once on all her stately gates
>   arose the answering fires . . .
> Till Belvoir's lordly terraces
>   the sign to Lincoln sent,
> And Lincoln sped the message on
>   o'er the wide vale of Trent;
> Till Skiddaw saw the fire that
>   burned on Gaunt's embattled pile,
> And the red glare on Skiddaw
>   roused the burghers of Carlisle.

The Queen also lit a torch to be flown to Australia to touch off a chain of three thousand bonfires there and witnessed on an immense screen the lighting of a bonfire in New Zealand by Sir Edmund Hillary. There was a beautiful display of fireworks, ending with the lighting-up of the emblem of the Queen's Silver Jubilee Appeal. The Queen spoke to spectators as she departed, expressing delight at the way the weather had been kind at the last minute, and the Prince of Wales declared an interest in having a taste of the ox which had been roasting with due ceremony for some time. Seventy thousand people had gathered in Windsor Great Park, and after the Queen had left, one of them was inspired to scale the Copper Horse to give a spirited rendering of 'Rule Britannia' to the universal delight of the crowd. His enthusiasm was too much for officialdom, however, and he was soon escorted to ground level.

In London that night, crowds contested cold, wet weather and long hours of waiting in order to ensure a good position on the processional route for the Queen's ceremonial drive to St. Paul's Cathedral the following day. The Jubilee spirit was everywhere, but as one policeman commented it did not seem to come from the bottle 'most of them are drinking tea as far as I can see. Everyone seems remarkably sober.' This contrasted favourably with the 1887 Jubilee of Queen Victoria, when R. D. Blumenfeld, in his day one of the best known figures in the newspaper world, confided in his diary 'I drove round London tonight

The Queen at Snow Hill, Windsor Great Park after lighting the first of a chain of bonfires on Monday 6 June.

in a curricle . . . I have never seen so many people; certainly never so many drunken ones'. Throughout the main Jubilee week in 1977 one of the lasting memories was the friendliness and warmth of the crowds.

Tuesday 7 June, which was a Bank Holiday in the United Kingdom, was a day of contrasts: first the panoply of a State occasion, followed by the informality of a walkabout, and then the Queen's address to the nation after lunch at the Guildhall.

The Jubilee procession was a considerably reduced version of the Coronation procession of 1953. Most Commonwealth countries were celebrating the Jubilee on home territory, reflecting the changing role of the Queen as Head of the Commonwealth. Now the Queen's one brow must wear eleven separate crowns, rather than one crown to which all nations are subject. Thus in 1977 the Queen made extensive tours of Commonwealth countries. However, the Royal Canadian Mounted Police, the ubiquitously popular 'Mounties' comprised part of the Queen's procession. At 10.25 am. Members of the Royal Family ranging in precedence from Princess Anne to Lord Mountbatten, left Buckingham Palace in six open carriages. They were accompanied by

London celebrating a royal occasion during the reign of Queen Victoria. An oil painting by William Holman Hunt.

a Captain's Escort of the Household Cavalry *without* Standard. Curiously of all the Royals, only Princess Margaret had been in the 1935 Jubilee procession and her outfit was reminiscent of the one she wore for her grandfather's festivities. Already seated in St. Paul's Cathedral was that veteran of royal occasions, Princess Alice, Countess of Athlone. She sat in quiet contemplation in the front row of the Cathedral, reflecting perhaps how very different things had become since she attended her grandmother's Diamond Jubilee service there some eighty years before.

The Royal Family's procession was followed closely by the procession of Queen Elizabeth the Queen Mother, accompanied owing to the niceties of precedence, by a Captain's Escort of the Household Cavalry *with* Standard. The Queen Mother travelled in the Irish State Coach with Prince Andrew, specially home from Canada for the week, and Prince Edward.

Finally, the Queen's procession left the Palace at 10.42 am. For the first time since the Coronation the Queen travelled in the Gold State Coach, built in 1762, and drawn by eight greys. She wore a rose-pink coat in soft silk crepe with wide-cuffed sleeves over a matching pleated dress. The hat matched the coat and had flowers dangling at the back. The Duke of Edinburgh wore the full dress uniform of Admiral of the Fleet, and as it was a 'collar day' the collar of the Order of the Garter.

Behind the coach rode the Prince of Wales in his full dress uniform of Colonel of Welsh Guards. He too wore the Collar of the Order of the Garter and the riband of the Order of the Thistle, to which he had been admitted during the Queen's visit to Edinburgh. Next came Sir John Miller, the Crown Equerry, who has overall responsibility for the

Members of the Royal Family arriving at St Paul's Cathedral. The Duke and Duchess of Kent watching the Earl of St Andrews, Lord Nicholas Windsor and Lady Helen Windsor alighting from their carriage.

Princess Alice, Countess of Athlone at the Silver Jubilee Royal Tournament on the day she broke the record as the oldest ever member of the British Royal Family, having lived 94 years and 140 days on 15 July 1977.

The Queen and the Duke of Edinburgh travelling in the Gold State Coach, and *below*, crowds watching the Queen's procession to St Paul's Cathedral.

coaches and horses, and the Master of the Horse, the Duke of Beaufort, who has held that office for forty years and is as old as the century. Four more carriages contained senior members of the Royal Household.

The route to St. Paul's Cathedral was thickly lined with crowds, sometimes twenty people deep. Fortunately during the Queen's procession the weather remained fair. In the Cathedral itself a fanfare announced the arrival of the Queen and a procession of clergy, heralds and the Lord Mayor bearing the Pearl Sword escorted the Queen, the Duke of Edinburgh and the Prince of Wales up the centre aisle while

The Officers of Arms leading the Queen's procession down the aisle of St Paul's Cathedral.

Opposite The Queen on her walkabout from St Paul's Cathedral to the Guildhall.

Below The Archbishop of Canterbury the Most Rev. and Rt. Hon. Donald Coggan.

the congregation sang 'All people that on earth do well'. As part of the service the Archbishop of Canterbury made an Address in which he compared the monarchy to a house built on firm foundations 'It is something at the heart of our national life of incalculable value – a spirit of devotion to duty and of service to others which has found its focus in a family and in a person'.

When the service had rolled through 'Immortal, invisible, God only wise', 'Praise my soul, the King of Heaven', an anthem, a prayer, the *Te Deum* and *The National Anthem*, the Queen and the Duke of Edinburgh processed from St. Paul's out into the sunlight and into the second part of their day.

This was the Queen's walk to the Guildhall, a chance for her to leave ceremony behind and have forty or so brief snippets of conversation with the crowd waiting along the route. The Queen, who had been solemn and dignified as befitted the great Service of Thanksgiving, now relaxed, smiled and was clearly enjoying herself. It was another example of the changing role of monarchy, in which the Queen is able to walk amongst her people without losing any of her mystique. 'Will I see the real Queen today?' one girl had asked her father. 'Now you can see that I'm real' said the Queen. Cries of all sorts rang out: 'Liz – you're a real beaut', 'Give us a kiss, Phil!' (he didn't) and banners were waved with slogans on them like 'Queen rules OK?' or more ingeniously 'Queen rules UK'.

'We have come here because we love you,' was one cry. 'I feel it and it means so much to me,' replied the Queen. 'Do you have a mechanical

arm to keep waving all the time, the way that you do?' – 'I haven't reached that stage yet', said the Queen. Brian Johnston, of the BBC, was quick to home in on those whose day had suddenly been made by a brisk chat with the Queen. He even got close enough to persuade Prince Philip to say a quick word into the microphone. So eager were the journalists for snippets of royal conversation that it was all too much for one little boy of eight. 'What did she say to you?' they asked. 'I forgot,' he replied.

At the Guildhall, the Queen and the immediate royal family sat down to lunch with the Lord Mayor of London. Television coverage of the day's events which had improved so much since the Coronation and was hailed in the *Daily Mail* as a 'spectacular electronic miracle', left the distinguished guests alone to have their lunch, but rejoined them for the speeches. The Lord Mayor spoke first and proposed the Queen's health. The Queen replied, emphasizing that the celebration of a Jubilee had undergone changes like everything else:

> In the olden days Jubilees were celebrated at the golden fiftieth year. The horns were sounded and a period of 'rest, mercy and pardon' was proclaimed. There was a distinct sabbatical flavour about the proceedings. It is beginning to dawn on me that a silver Jubilee is of a somewhat different nature! But if this is not exactly a period of rest for us, it is certainly one of refreshment and of happiness and satisfaction.

The Queen ended her speech by looking back on the speech she made in South Africa in 1947:

> My Lord Mayor, when I was twenty-one, I pledged my life to the service of our people and I asked for God's help to make good that vow. Although that vow was made 'in my salad days when I was green in judgement' I do not regret nor retract one word of it!

The Queen in her 'salad days' making her pledge in a broadcast in Cape Town on 21 April 1947.

After lunch the royal family returned to Buckingham Palace in another procession of carriages amidst an estimated one million people. The Queen and the Duke appeared on the balcony of the Palace, and the Mall was entirely filled by the crowd. Whenever they went in, a repeated cry of 'We want the Queen, We want the Queen' was chanted. The throngs of friendly and loyal subjects were rewarded by several more balcony appearances. When the crowds finally drifted away, still some youths remained singing 'Land of Hope and Glory'.

The following day, which dawned brightly for the 30,000 recipients of the Queen's Silver Jubilee medal, was somewhat quieter for the Queen. There were more Commonwealth Heads of Government to receive and in the evening a Dinner Party for all those attending the conference. Amongst the guests were well-known statesmen such as Archbishop Makarios of Cyprus, shortly before his sudden death, Dr. Kenneth Kaunda of Zambia, Lee Kuan Yew of Singapore, Pierre Trudeau of Canada and Malcolm Fraser of Australia.

The Prince of Wales, Prince Edward, Princess Anne, Earl Mountbatten of Burma, The Queen, The Duke of Edinburgh, Princess Margaret, Prince Andrew and The Queen Mother on the Balcony of Buckingham Palace on 7 June.

On Thursday 9 June the Queen had the longest day of the Jubilee celebrations. She and the Duke of Edinburgh embarked on the *Nore* at Greenwich at 10.30 am and proceeded up river to Lambeth. They made various stops en route visiting the Pepys Estate at Deptford, Cherry Garden Pier and Southwark Park, and calling in at St. Katharine's Dock. At Deptford, the Queen met Mrs Florence Stead who had met Queen Victoria during her Jubilee in 1887. Mrs Stead, who thought the Queen was 'lovely', was 100 years old. Then they embarked in the Royal Barge and proceeded to the Upper Pool of London where *Britannia* was waiting for them. They held a lunch party and guests included the Prime Minister and Mrs Callaghan. At 3 pm. they set off in the *Nore* and proceeded to Lambeth Pier. The Queen reviewed the London Fire Brigade and took tea with the Archbishop of Canterbury.

In the evening the Queen arrived at Westminster Bridge and unveiled a plaque on the South Bank Lion to officially open the Silver Jubilee Walkway, the new five and a quarter-mile walk from Leicester Square to Tower Hill. From County Hall, she watched an illuminated pageant of more than a hundred boats dressed overall with messages of congratulation.

The weather took a turn for the worse as dusk fell, but the crowds continued to gather. The Queen walked along the South Bank to the Jubilee Gardens, where she unveiled a plaque to mark their opening. The Jubilee Gardens, on the site of the Festival Hall Car Park, were specially designed to mark the occasion. Then she joined other members

Left The Royal Yacht *Britannia* arriving in the Upper Pool London to take part in the Queen's River Progress 9 June.

Right The Prime Minister and Mrs Callaghan returning from *Britannia* after lunching with the Queen.

Far right The Queen's Bargemaster and one of the Watermen on the Royal Barge.

Below right The Queen and the Duke of Edinburgh on the Royal Barge.

Below Crowds lining the Thames for the Queen's River Progress.

of the Royal Family in the Shell Building to watch the most magnificent display of fireworks London has ever seen.

No one who saw the thousands of coloured lights that exploded heavenwards will ever forget how London's sky was transformed. Amidst the cascades, some 'mortars' were driven so high into the clouds that they had time to be forgotten before bursting into a new display far above the rest. There were simultaneous displays at Crystal Palace, Alexandra Palace, Greenwich, Richmond and from barges moored opposite the Jubilee Gardens. The half-hour display, choreographed by John Piper and Rev Ron Lancaster, was seen by television viewers the world over.

After the display the Queen and the Royal Family drove back to the Palace in carriages. London traffic ground to a halt, but nobody seemed to mind as the friendly crowds surged towards Buckingham Palace to

The Prince of Wales joking with waiters in the Shell Building where the Royal Family gathered to watch the fireworks.

Right and opposite The Thames alight with fireworks on 9 June.

The Queen and Prince Andrew leaving the Shell Building in the Irish State Coach after the fireworks display.

see the Queen on the balcony. Such crowds had not been seen since VE night. They sang 'Jerusalem', they sang 'Maybe it's because I'm a Londoner' and they cried out 'We want the Queen'. There was a general feeling of euphoria, shared by the people and the police who also joined in the singing. So friendly were the crowds that anyone who had to reach a specific destination could brush their way through. They were in striking contrast to the football crowds who make headlines through violence and vandalism.

Friday was described as a quiet day for the Queen, quiet only in comparison to Tuesday and Thursday. The Queen held fourteen audiences and an evening party for the staffs of Commonwealth delegations. Saturday was her official birthday and the crowds gathered once more for the Birthday Parade and RAF fly past. On Sunday and Monday she was at Windsor for a march past of British Legion Standards and the Garter ceremony.

The Queen still had three major engagements in London with a specifically Jubilee flavour, though in the privacy of the Palace the Privileged Bodies presented addresses on 1 and 8 July. On 30 June the Queen made her South London Drive, stopping at various points including Wandsworth Municipal Buildings and the GLC Foxley Estate where she unveiled a seat for elderly residents. One Mayor on the route received a certain amount of opposition within the council for welcoming the Queen. 'So I put on my full robes, which was a popular gesture,' he said proudly.

In the evening she arrived by carriage at the Empire Stadium, Wembley to review Reserve and Cadet Forces and watched the Services

The Queen on her South London Drive on 30 June.

Above The Queen at the Geffrye Museum with curator Jeffery Daniels during her North London Drive on 6 July.

Left and below Crowds awaiting the Queen on the North London Drive.

A Pearly King watching the Queen's car.

Silver Jubilee Musical Pageant. On 6 July it was North London's turn. The Queen visited the Geffrye Museum to see the exhibition 'Lousy but Loyal' and drove through Camden, Islington, Hackney and Tower Hamlets. On both the drives it was the children and their mothers who formed the majority of the crowds. The children were really keen to see the Queen and such a long route meant that it was easy to get a view of her. One little boy in Hackney was asked by his mother, 'Have you got a flag?' 'I've got two,' he replied.

As the Queen entered Buckingham Palace at the end of her North London drive, her Silver Jubilee engagements in London came to an end.

The Queen driving home with some of the bunches of flowers given to her during her drive.

ER
HOTEL
WOODVILLE HOUSE
VACANCIES

London Celebrates

The Queen driving from London Airport after returning from Kenya in February 1952, following the death of King George VI.

Left One of the many individual decorations to be seen in London.

Early in 1976 when the word came 'no expenditure on the rates', confusion reigned in the Boroughs on the frantic issue – to celebrate or not to celebrate. Headlines in local papers varied from 'Don't spend our money on Jubilee' and 'Let's all celebrate '77' to the more general 'Wait and see policy on Queen's Jubilee'. The residents of Mirabel Road, Fulham, started raising money as early as August 1975 by levying a voluntary 15p per household every Friday. By June they had raised £350 of the hoped-for £1,000, had booked a discotheque for the day and were planning three parties. 'We may be a small street, but we think big,' commented a committee member.

Some Boroughs wanted to ignore the Jubilee all together. 'It's irrelevant when one considers our local education cuts, rate support grants, and unemployment amongst Borough officers and staff.' Others were full of enthusiasm, for example, Hillingdon, at one time the only GLC Borough planning a big celebration with a special excuse for doing it: 'Our Borough was the first the new Queen touched down on upon landing from Kenya in 1952'. Some were vociferous against it all: 'We're the Borough that turns the Queen's picture round in the Town Hall at Council meetings'. There were ominous words from Barking: 'We're the only Borough to have got away with not celebrating the Festival of Britain or the Coronation and we don't intend starting now.'

An enthusiast whose early efforts did much to stir up the Boroughs was Leslie Hilliard, Chairman of the General Purposes Committee of the London Boroughs Association. He addressed the Mayors at a meeting in the Banqueting House in June 1976 and made the vital point that every citizen would be able to celebrate the Jubilee in whatever way he wished. 'What we want to see is London *en fête*,' he urged.

It was far from simple to support the Jubilee at the local level with no public money, without giving the impression of supporting it too actively, which might ignite the anti-members of the Council, or indeed too passively, which would bring local Young Conservatives and umbrella-waving royalists to their feet. Everyone approached it

Archers and Morris Dancers at Bexley.

differently. Hammersmith of which Leslie Hilliard happened also to be Mayor, declared 'this Borough is going to blaze with loyalty from end to end', whereas Camden claimed to have merely 'a sorting office for imaginative ideas'. Committees stated 'We're not doing anything really just trying to help the enthusiasts here'. Some announced with confidence 'We've got our most powerful men on this Committee' and others, plaintively 'Nobody really wants to organise events here, have you got any ideas?'. Some committees were set up by the Council with its blessing but no money or suggestions, others were set up despite the Council; some maintained low profiles, and some even had to appeal for local volunteers to set up *ad hoc* groups of their own. It varied from thoroughly established committees to small groups, themselves burning with enthusiasm but struggling valiantly against all sorts of political undercurrents. One of the *ad hoc* organisers was Fred Clarke of Haringey, the brother of novelist Arthur C. Clarke. He ran the celebrations from his own front room out of sheer love for the Queen. Then there was the West London Councillor, a broad cockney and a thoroughly lovable character who, arriving late at meetings would excuse himself briskly 'I'm sorry to be forty-five minutes late, but I'm a bit like that sometimes'. At his local Jubilee Banquet, he rose to his feet to welcome guests with the words 'How about getting on with the bloody food?'

The London Celebrations Committee injected £1,000 into each Borough to help stimulate activity. They did this on condition that a representative committee had been set up and that evidence was provided to prove it was receiving some other support, preferably financial, in the area.

They also injected Tom Petzal recently of the Welsh National Opera and Drama Company as a roving advisor to help those Boroughs which were not quite certain how to join in the fun. Tom Petzal defined his role as 'to be able to know where to lay my hands on anything at a moment's notice. You want an orchestra or an elephant? Come to me.' His actual title was Borough Liaison Executive which in every Borough meant something different. 'Are you purely seconded to Waltham Forest?' he was asked. 'How many liaison officers are there in this part of London?' or 'Is the celebrations Committee a part of the GLC or was it set up by the Royal Family?'

When introduced to Borough Committees Petzal faced a barrage of questions – 'If he's there, why are we?' – 'What does he think of our annual darts competition?', and the ever popular one 'Who pays him?' He became a habitué of these meetings – the world of ideas being created and minuted, the minutes being read, amended, and approved – and he enjoyed the pattern. There was still a fair deal of caution in the air though. 'Is he taking notes? If so I don't want to be on record.'

In this way the idea of carnivals, fêtes, donkey derbies, *It's a knockout* competitions, Elizabethan Fayres and other entertainments began to

A Jubilee Street in London filled with balloons and streamers on the Jubilee weekend and both old and young enjoying themselves.

grip the public imagination. Borough events were separate from street parties, of course, each street party having its own organising committee. They often wanted distinguished celebrities to open theirs, ranging from André Previn and Dame Alicia Markova to Led Zeppelin and David Bowie. They also hoped that the liaison executive might perhaps be the man who 'supplied the booze'. In this, at least, they were disappointed.

Public meetings to discuss the local plans also produced a wide variety of stimulating ideas from the floor. Islington wanted to have Oktoberfests in Finsbury Park, Hampstead made a plea for fireworks with the Queen's head, and Tower Hamlets suggested a torchlight procession round Jack the Ripper's Walk. Hillingdon called for the London Symphony Orchestra or the English Chamber Orchestra to visit them at last, and Hounslow invited Angela Rippon (who declined). Local personalities were in great demand. Hounslow boasted Richard Attenborough in the vicinity and hoped he would put on a show. Hammersmith had three top grade League Football clubs and proposed that George Best might read 'Peter and the Wolf' to the kids. Just as local personalities were sought, so the Boroughs tended to be insular. Entertainments were to be home run and for the benefit of local residents. Certainly, anyone who visited a street party of a different area got the impression that they were in some way intruding. This feeling was voiced early on: 'If the masque is at Chiswick, nobody in Feltham or Heston will be interested' and 'You can't expect the Hampstead crowd to be Camden orientated – they're all intellectuals'.

Local fund raising was a different affair from the central effort. The outgoing Mayor of one of the Boroughs became the centre of a 'guess the weight of the Mayor' competition. This was very successful as that particular Mayor, though a huge man weighing some fifteen stone, was of a retiring disposition and not widely known in the Borough. A general error (and from a fund-raising point of view a very welcome one) was that a number of residents tried to size up the new Mayor, a man of somewhat slenderer proportions.

Some men proved to be 'starters' but not 'finishers'. One Councillor of right-wing leanings would promise everything and do nothing. 'You can count on me. I'll push it through' soon became a warning that nothing would be done. Other battle cries he was accustomed to utter before going into retreat were 'we must get a bit of adrenalin into the young fellows around here', 'We've got no money, but a lot of willing workers to put their backs into it', and more ominously 'You must come round for a drink one evening and we'll chat about it'.

Hounslow gave a banquet to raise funds in the style proved admirably successful by President Jimmy Carter. Tickets were sold at £25 each, and former Rank Chief Executive Graham Dowson made an uplifting speech. In Newham a Jubilee *dance* competition was planned. A local councillor misunderstood this and wound himself into a state of total

A relay race with a difference. The blind-folded participant about to burst the balloon and the runner attempting to catch the water in the cup and getting somewhat damp in the process.

A lady wearing a Union Jack hat she made herself.

bewilderment as to why a *darts* competition had to take place in an unlicenced outdoor stadium seating twenty thousand and, what's more, in the early afternoon.

Even at the beginning of 1977, it was far from certain that the Jubilee would take off. Newspapers echoed the general feeling, of which this item in the *Evening Standard* is typical: 'We are scarcely into 1977 yet, but already everybody is looking pretty shell-shocked in the ceaseless barrage of Jubilee propaganda, nostalgia and exploitation. . . .' The change from scepticism to enthusiasm more or less coincided with the Queen's return to London at the beginning of May, following her Australian tour and a brief holiday. The media as a whole began to respond to the atmosphere which was beginning to grip the country. Both local and national papers became very enthusiastic, and started to ask what was going to happen.

On 6 May announcements were made about local plans and it became clear that Jubilee fever had reached epidemic proportions. Around the Boroughs there grew a willingness to help. Organisations like the Townswomens Guilds, the Rotary Clubs and the Royal British Legion began to give valuable support. Suddenly the political recalcitrance that pervaded many Town Halls was replaced by a zest to be involved. The Jubilee became fashionable. Even the people of Barking, whose

Right and below 'A Merrie England'.

'The Wash House' by Ron Barnes of Stepney exhibited in the London Naive Painters' exhibition, part of the Greater London Picture Show.

Council had been roundly castigated by the *Evening Standard* for its 'churlish behaviour' in not supporting the Jubilee, suddenly decided they loved it. The Borough had its first concert ever. The Barking Arts Council staged 'Merrie England' Edward German's nostalgic tribute to Elizabeth I, on the very steps of the Town Hall, with the audience seated ironically on council chairs. It was described locally as 'the greatest cultural event to hit Barking'. Ten other special events celebrated the Jubilee there. One was the Dagenham Town Show, with horses and sheep-shearing, which was self-styled as 'the finest show in the South of England'. Two hundred and thirty-three streets were closed for street happenings in the Borough during the Jubilee period, which represented a minimum number (other parties taking place in schools and already enclosed areas). The popular response in Barking was generally deemed a major break-through.

It is estimated that over 3,000 people were directly or indirectly involved in organising Borough events. Over 650,000 people of all ages were actually participating (performing, making cakes or putting up street decorations). Quite apart from the hundreds of thousands who

The Havering Jubilee Pack.

A 1935 street party in Merchant Street, from the East End exhibition *Lousy but Loyal*.

turned up for the fun on the day, this means that one in twelve of the entire population of London had been sufficiently bitten by Jubilee fever to do something about it. The Boroughs boasted 5,000 street happenings and 2,000 other events to celebrate the Queen. Havering, who topped the list of street happenings with at least 492, sold Jubilee packs containing badges, tee-shirts, streamers and balloons. At six pounds a pack, they have sold 40,000 to date.

Boroughs such as Hounslow, Redbridge, Waltham Forest, Havering and Brent staged exhibitions to show the changing face of their Borough in a series of photographs. The Greater London Picture Show was the largest ever Borough exhibition and travelled round London in the course of the summer, being hung everywhere from the most refined of art galleries to the walls of public swimming baths. Contributors ranged from David Hockney to members of the general public. London's naïve artists, united to present their view of London. Stanley Harries was the successful organiser of the show. He claimed to be an amateur: 'Really I know nothing about pictures or hanging them, I just have a bit of taste.' One day he went down to the Whitechapel Art Gallery to look for material for the exhibition before it went to Olympia. There he met Ron Barnes, a 45-year-old cab driver who had written one successful book and been given an Arts Council grant of £500 to enable him to write another. He told Harries the pictures were 'all rubbish'. Then he said: 'You got a moment?' So began a five-mile trek to the nether regions of the East End, Harries motoring behind his bicycle. When they reached his abode, Ron Barnes dismounted and called upstairs, 'Doll, I've got a bloke to see the paintings. Fix 'im a cuppa.' Harries then found himself face to face with about forty or fifty wonderful paintings of life in the East End. He took some at once to Olympia and they got the best mention in a review by the *New York Herald Tribune*.

Tower Hamlets put on their first ever exhibition of paintings by old age pensioners. This came about because at the very first Jubilee gathering at Bethnal Green Town Hall an old man rose to his feet and challenged the assembled company with the question 'Anyone know who painted the picture of the Queen down in the front foyer?' An ignorant hush fell in the chamber. 'Well I bloody did,' he went on, and then launched into an impassioned plea not to neglect the old folks, which culminated in their exhibition.

Lousy but Loyal, the Geffrye Museum's exhibition, which was visited by the Queen on her North London Drive, collected a wide range of material showing how the East End had celebrated previous Jubilees. The title came from a banner seen in one of the photographs.

Famous stars toured the Boroughs on floats on the bank holiday weekend of 6 and 7 June. Rolf Harris, Patrick Moore, Vera Lynn ('She's really the only one in that lot who means anything to our Borough') and others entertained anyone who cared to come along. It certainly was not the weather which brought out the crowds. Yet despite constant drizzle the show went on regardless. Sometimes things went awry: for example, Cliff Richard stood disconsolately at one end of his Borough while his float searched for him in vain at the other.

Music was so much in demand that Chappells Music vans raced all over London to meet tight performance deadlines and fill important gaps in musical productions. The English Chamber Orchestra did visit Hillingdon, their concert inaugurating the Alfred Beck Theatre. The Prince of Wales rode a bicycle on stage at the opening of the Churchill Theatre in Bromley, *Belshazzar's Feast* was digested at the Wembley Conference Centre and the Queen's Theatre Hornchurch heard its first ever *Messiah*.

Wembley had a Jewish concert, the only one of its type, Lambeth and Wandsworth had steel bands, Ealing had Indian music and the Banqueting House, Whitehall had the Bloomsbury Society's *Dark and Delicious* with readings from Susannah York, dancing and playing, conducting and organising by Ian Hall, who persuaded all but the most reluctant members of the audience onto their feet and into the swing of things. The Bubble Theatre's *Queen's Silver Jubilee Show* about their Sovereign claimed by the name of 'Elizabeth of Hammersmith' (or wherever it was) went to fourteen different Boroughs revelling in a year of 'celebration, expansion, excitement and mystique'. The programme was launched in Hackney, which also staged a Silver Jubilee Cockney Show.

Clapham put on a steam traction rally and Ilford sponsored several Jubilee plays at the Kenneth More Theatre. On 19 June a Festival of Early Music was held at the Hall Place Estate, Crayford in Bexley. Lutes were played and madrigals sung to a record-breaking audience of 15,000 people, many of whom wore Elizabethan tophats. The success of the event was proved by a chaotic traffic jam on the A2 and the trampling of the estate's flower beds as the audience crowded to get a better view. Bexley were enthusiastic about the festival and hope to make it an annual affair.

Other boroughs have become inspired to repeat the fun of this year. Hillingdon intend to re-invite the English Chamber Orchestra next year and are also investing in more concerts. Havering have plans for a series of adult and children's concerts in 1978. The Greater London Picture Show has resulted in an awareness about naïve art in the capital, and plans are already afoot for a permanent centre for naïve artists in the middle of town. Barking enjoyed their *Merrie England* so much that they are keen to have another patriotic concert next year.

Today when Tom Petzal meets a Mayor from one of the Boroughs who were slow to start planning their junketings, he chides him good-naturedly. The Mayor invariably scratches the back of his neck and mutters something about 'teething problems' but will soon switch the conversation to the fun they had and the plans they are considering for the future.

Rolf Harris standing beside his float on Monday 6 June.

SUN XIX
LONDON
SUN XIX
VIC 32

A confrontation between The Queen and Dame Edna Everage (*alias* Barry Humphries) at the Royal Windsor Big Top Show on 28 May.

In 1977 it was possible for everyone to celebrate in their own way. Those who liked music and theatre had special treats, those who preferred more rugged pursuits could indulge them too. Prince Philip himself declared that the Jubilee was a good excuse for a party. More than that it was also an excuse to get some things done which had needed doing for a long time.

The Thames, described by Max Nicholson as 'the spine of London' came into its own in 1977. Tony Bell stood by Tower Bridge and observed three hundred racing dinghies wending their way down river to the Tower of London and exclaimed 'that's what Jubilees are all about, everyone enjoying themselves'. Observing the dinghies, it seemed as though one had been transported to Hong Kong harbour as the multi-coloured sails vied with each other for first place. The six hundred competitors beached their boats nearby and repaired to the moat of the Tower of London. In that historic setting, the shades of some of its former inmates observed with envy the serving of a lavish seafood picnic, washed down with ale. In the circumstances, the return race must have been all the more challenging. At Putney, Princess Anne was awaiting the winners to present a well-earned prize.

The Jubilee Tideway race was but one of an extensive programme of river events. As London's river loses importance as a commercial thoroughfare its recreational possibilities are beginning to be explored. The major problem of the Thames was the rubbish and pieces of timber

The highly decorated barge which started the Jubilee Tideway Race

OCL

989
2976
E
K9654
E
7285
903
F
1638

Princess Anne at Putney for the prize-giving for the Jubilee Tideway Race.

Left Dinghies on the Thames in the Jubilee Tideway Race on 9 July.

Left Sailing barges taking part in the Thames Sailing Barge and Smack Race and Rally on 4 June.

which came and went according to the tide. To trap the passing driftwood, a new environmental boom was constructed which can be placed across the Thames wherever needed.

The river events were inaugurated on 17 May when the Lord Mayor hoisted the London Jubilee flag on HMS *Belfast*. Tower Bridge opened and barges with flags at their mastheads sailed into the Upper Pool of London. This was the sign for the mass unfurling of Jubilee flags all along the river. The central part of the river events was, of course, the Queen's progress from Greenwich to Lambeth. However a great number of competitions were also organised with the emphasis on having fun rather than winning.

One such was the Marlboro Jubilee Cup International Power Boat Meeting between Albert and Chelsea Bridges on 2 and 3 July. The Thames became for the first time in recent history a deafening race track with all the excitement of a major race, some boats pulling into the pits in moments of crisis, and others sinking. The speed with which the boats were repaired was astonishing and the lead changed hands several times before the end of each race. Princess Margaret started the Formula 1 (OZ, ON, OI Class) race on 3 July, which included the

The Lord Mayor of London, Sir Robin Gillett, hoisting the Jubilee flag on HMS *Belfast* on 17 May.

A competitor heading towards Battersea Bridge in the Marlboro Jubilee Cup International Powerboat Meeting on 2 July.

Princess Margaret alighting from *Nore* at Battersea Park on 3 July.

European Endurance Championship Heat, and got so close to the action on Battersea Pier that she was soaked by the Gordon's Gin Cougar. The races were such a success that they should be repeated.

On 21 May there was a yacht race from off the entrance to the Meadway to Tower Bridge with many ocean racers competing and Jubilee Eights raced each evening from 12 to 14 July between London Bridge and Westminster. The Port of London River Services Display took place on 12 and 13 August. At one point a well-planned fire of lurid orange smoke broke out on the Port of London Authority vessel *Crossness*. This caused some consternation in the commentary box, when it failed to go out on schedule, and the commentary box itself disappeared into the general haze.

In contrast to the street parties in the Boroughs were two happenings in Berkeley Square on 5 and 7 July. The first was a party for all those who worked in and around the region of the Square. An old-fashioned programme was issued for this 'Mayfair' as 'an accurate Defcription and Profpect of the Sunday Booths, Pavilions, Pleasances, Revels and Musick situated among the Parades and Arbours of the said Square'. Prince Michael of Kent opened the festivities as Patron of the Berkeley Square Silver Jubilee Association, and guests were then confronted with the chance to try their skills at rowing, golf, apple bobbing, and such rare pursuits as shaving balloons.

Two nights later, on 7.7.77, the Bond Street Ball was held in aid of the Queen's Silver Jubilee Appeal to celebrate both the Jubilee and the once a century date. Twenty-five pounds was the price of a double-ticket and a further twenty-five pounds secured a raffle ticket and the chance to take home a 1952 Rolls-Royce. Appropriately a piped nightingale sang in the Square to greet the guests who included David Bailey, Mick Jagger and David Essex. Lord Lichfield, with Princess Margaret on his arm, mounted the stage at eleven o'clock to propose a loyal toast to the Queen. There were strawberries and cream and champagne in tents, and topless dancers on the stage. On one of the warmest nights of the year, George Melly belted out the 1920 blues and guests danced to steel bands under an open canopy. Lord Lichfield and Mr. Fish (of shirt fame, and Chairman of the Ball) spent £21 on the tombola at £1 a go until Princess Margaret won a prize. When she left at two in the morning she had it with her – a ship in a glass bottle. The party carried on until the sun had firmly risen, several policemen had been relieved of their helmets by eager debutantes, and some of the guests retreated home with the distinct feeling that the Queen's Silver Jubilee had been all too worthily celebrated.

Two major contributions came from Lord Delfont. The first was EMI's film, '25 Years – Impressions', which was released in February. The Prince of Wales attended its premiere, arriving to a fanfare of trumpets. The documentary included scenes of the Queen's recent visit to Boston and gave an amusing insight into the chaotic prepara-

Above left Prince Michael of Kent trying his luck at a game of tiddlywinks in Berkeley Square on 5 July.

Above A Policeman and a guest dancing happily into the night at the Bond Street Ball in Berkeley Square on 7 July.

Left The 'Mayfair' in full swing on 5 July.

Right The Earl of Lichfield and Michael Fish with Princess Margaret after her success on the tombola at the Bond Street Ball on 7 July 1977.

group

tions that herald such an occasion. It also looked back over the twenty-five years of the Queen's reign and showed the Queen and the Royal Family in holiday mood at Balmoral.

Another spectacular from Lord Delfont was 'Night of 100 Stars' attended by Princess Alexandra at the National Theatre on Sunday, 22 May. Well-known stars of the past twenty-five years and earlier gathered at either side of the stage to sip celebratory champagne and witness excerpts from opera, variety, Shakespeare, music hall, theatre and dancing. The walk-on parts were taken by household names and even the programme sellers were well known personalities, such as Honor Blackman. Kenneth More introduced the stars, who included Jack Hulbert and Cicely Courtneidge, John Clements and Kay Hammond, Jessie Mathews, Rod Hull and Emu, Danny La Rue, Glenda Jackson and David Nixon. Johnnie Dankworth, John Williams, Stephane Grapelli and Cleo Laine provided music and song, and Dame Wendy Hiller spoke the epilogue. One member of the audience attempted to count the stars and joked that if there weren't a hundred he'd 'have Lord Delfont under the Trade Descriptions Act'. This spectacular was shown on Independent Television during the Jubilee weekend. Unfortunately Lord Delfont's other hope – that he might reunite the Beatles for the first time since 1969 for a pop-concert at Wembley – proved impossible.

London has always enjoyed a healthy cultural life. Thus the effect of the Jubilee was to top up existing musical programmes and to give a number of these a Jubilee slant. Enthusiasts for royal music had a heyday, and a league table of the most often performed works in 1977 reads as follows:

1. 'Merrie England'
2. 'Zadok the Priest'
3. 'My Heart is Inditing'
4. 'I was Glad'
5. 'Blessed Pair of Sirens'

The London Orchestras gave the Jubilee a royal send-off. The Royal Philharmonic celebrated by returning to their base at Croydon to perform under the baton of that doyen of British conductors Sir Charles Groves. André Previn began the London Symphony Orchestra's concert with John McCabe's *Jubilee Prelude*, commissioned by the London Celebrations Committee. A rather special facet of the L.P.O. programme was their Festival Hall concert in which Sir Georg Solti in a jubilee concert conducted Elgar's 2nd Symphony in the Queen Mother's presence.

The London Celebrations Committee commissioned other new works to mark the Jubilee. Cultural Programme Chairman, John Denison commented: 'In deciding which British composers we should approach we were strongly influenced by a desire to provide pieces which could

Penelope Keith in a 'Night of 100 Stars'.

Kenneth More introducing Jack Hulbert and Cicely Courtneidge at 'Night of 100 Stars' at the National Theatre on 22 May.

be played, sung and enjoyed by as many participants as possible'. On 5 June at Covent Garden Mr. Denison himself took part in one of them, skilfully tackling the triangle in the Jubilee Toy Symphony, a jubilant piece for piano, strings and toy instruments by Joseph Horovitz. Others on stage with conductor Colin Davis, included Yehudi Menuhin, who blew a whistle, Richard Baker, who played a quail, and a host of other celebrities battling with cuckoos, toy drums and cymbals. The concert, *Jubilee Jeunesse*, was a Youth and Music gala to honour the Queen and fete the 98th birthday of its founder, Sir Robert Mayer. Sir Robert was present, sporting a white dinner jacket and carnation and clearly enjoying himself immensely. He stood up in the Royal Box and waved with gusto to the audience, all of whom look forward to his centennial concert (already booked). The talented young musicians who performed were introduced by famous name's from the world of music.

Richard Rodney Bennett was commissioned to write a Serenade for Youth Orchestra which was first heard at the Royal Albert Hall on 24 April and simultaneously performed by youth orchestras in fourteen London boroughs. On the same occasion John Rutter's *Jubilee Unison Song*, a carol for children, was sung. During the main Jubilee week the Albert Hall was taken over by Victor Hochhauser and Harold Holt for

The Band of the Royal Green Jackets marching 160 steps to the minute at Royal Albert Hall on 7 June.

Malcolm Williamson (Master of the Queen's Music), Anne Murray, John Denison, Nigel Kennedy and Richard Rodney Bennett rehearsing the Jubilee Toy Symphony at Covent Garden on 5 June.

a series of Royal Silver Jubilee Concerts. On the day of the Thanksgiving Service, there was a Military Bands Spectacular entitled *Homage to The Queen.* The performance included Elgar's *Coronation Ode* set to music for the coronation of King Edward VII in which *Land of Hope and Glory* appears in its original form. The specially commissioned *English Dance Suite* by John Gardner received its first performance.

The choir and military bands numbered over 400 performers while the entire floor of the Royal Albert Hall was used for displays including the memorable double-time marching from the Royal Green Jackets at 160 paces to the minute. Lt.-Col. Trevor Sharpe, one of the finest all-round musicians ever to grace a military establishment, looked back on the pageantry of the royal day and pointed out that a number of the musicians had been on duty on the processional route. 'They've been out in the streets,' he said.

On 11 June it was the turn of the Massed Brass Bands, a chance for London to hear the best bands from the industrial cities, for example, the Black Dyke Mills Band and Foden's Motor Works Band. Harry Mortimer, OBE, now aged 75, came back to conduct. He had directed a band at the time of the Festival of Britain. William Mathias's piece *Vivat Regina*, a suite for Brass Band, was performed for the first time.

The museums of London staged many special exhibitions during 1977. 'London and the Thames – Paintings of three centuries' was a unique exhibition which was visited by the Queen Mother on 6 July at Somerset House. The exhibition occupied the Fine Rooms, some of which had not been seen publicly since the early 1800s. The Fine Rooms

Opposite The Queen Mother and Baroness Birk in the Fine Rooms of Somerset House at the Opening of 'London and the Thames' on 6 July.

were restored to their former splendour and filled with a colourful series of paintings which showed the changing face of London's river over three centuries through the eyes of Canaletto, Constable, Gainsborough, Kokoshka, Monet, Sisley, Turner, Whistler, and other artists. Many of the paintings had travelled an exceptionally long way to get there, journeys fraught with the inevitable problems of transporting a priceless old master overseas. The Smithsonian Institute in Washington was one lender, and other pictures came from public and private collections in Australia, Western Europe and even from the Eastern Bloc. The exhibition was open until October.

The National Portrait Gallery put on *Happy and Glorious* which covered 130 years of photographs of and by members of the Royal Family. *This Brilliant Year* at the Royal Academy took a retrospective look at the 1887 celebrations of Queen Victoria's Jubilee. The title took its inspiration from a note in her journal: 'Never, never can I forget this brilliant year, so full of the marvellous kindness, loyalty, and devotion of so many millions, which really I could hardly have expected'. In the exhibition were paintings, water-colours, prints, photographs, books, sculpture, coins and medals. One portrait group by Laurits Tuxen showed Queen Victoria at Windsor in 1887, surrounded by fifty-five members of her family. To the fore is a small girl in a party-frock, today the only survivor of the group, Princess Alice, Countess of Athlone. The exhibition also provided a chance to see the original sailor suit worn by Albert Edward, Prince of Wales (later Edward VII) in the 1846 portrait by Winterhalter.

The Commemorative Collectors Society staged *Jubilee Royal* at the Goldsmiths' Hall, which was opened by Princess Alice, Duchess of Gloucester on 10 May. It traced the origins and history of Royal Jubilees from the earliest time to the present day through the field of commemoratives. The exhibition later travelled to Edinburgh, Cardiff and Sheffield. Madame Tussaud's presented a new royal group in wax and the Horniman Museum displayed some of the extraordinary articles given to the Royal Family on their travels overseas under the title *Travellers Royal*.

Battersea Park was the venue for two exciting endeavours, the British Genius Exhibition and a Silver Jubilee Exhibition of British Sculpture. British Genius traced Britain's achievements over the past century in the fields of science, technology, literature, art, theatre, music, sport and dress, and suggested ways in which British genius is finding many answers for the future. The Duke of Edinburgh sent a message to its sponsors, the John Player Foundation in which he described the achievements of the past century as 'probably the most prolific output by any nation at any time'. The Duke added an optimistic note and a warning: 'That this genius has not dried up is demonstrated by the number of brilliant ideas of our own generation, but if they are to flourish they must be planted in a fertile soil.' The Sculpture exhibi-

The Duke of Edinburgh, followed by Neville Labovitch, about to witness weight lifting at the Silver Jubilee Exhibition in Hyde Park on 30 June.

Left Fabergé pieces from the Royal Collection at Sandringham on display at the Victoria and Albert Museum from June to October. Reproduced by gracious permission of Her Majesty The Queen.

Right Queen Victoria surrounded by her family at Windsor in 1887. The little girl in the foreground is Princess Alice, Countess of Athlone. The painting by Laurits Tuxen, hung in 'This Brilliant Year' at the Royal Academy is reproduced by gracious permission of Her Majesty The Queen.

Albert Edward, Prince of Wales, in the dress of a British Sailor, a portrait by Winterhalter, from 'This Brilliant Year' Reproduced by gracious permission of Her Majesty The Queen.

tion included works by Henry Moore, Barbara Hepworth and forty-three other contemporary British sculptors.

Towards the end of June a massive tent began to appear in Hyde Park. This was the BP tent designed for the inauguration of the Forties Oil Field in Aberdeen in 1975. It housed the Silver Jubilee Exhibition, the inspiration of Neville Labovitch, an exhibition which demonstrated the achievement and potential of British industry and commerce. One of the highlights especially on particularly hot days was the igloo in which visitors were submitted to Alaskan temperatures by means of special refrigeration and the sound of driving winds in order to give them some idea of the conditions in which BP are carrying out drilling operations in Prudhoe Bay. This igloo was hailed as 'the coldest spot in The Capital'. Thirty-one public and private sector companies took part in the exhibition, the first in Hyde Park since the Great Exhibition of 1851.

From early each morning and throughout each day, queues extended as far as Exhibition Road to inspect the collection of Fabergé pieces at the Victoria and Albert museum, many of which came from Sandringham. Graham Sutherland's portraits were shown together as a collection for the first time, appropriately twenty-five years since he undertook his greatest commission, the Coventry tapestry.

Lord Hunt reunited with the model of Everest at the Royal Geographical Society on 20 June.

Westminster Cathedral ablaze with flowers on 30 June.

Other events took on a Silver Jubilee flavour such as the Royal Tournament, an annual happening which suddenly became the 'Silver Jubilee Royal Tournament'. In case one had missed it on television, the film of 'The Life and Times of Lord Mountbatten' was shown in twelve instalments at the Imperial War Museum. At the Royal Geographical Society, lectures were given in June on the subject 'Exploration during the Queen's Reign'. Lord Hunt, who led the Everest Expedition in 1953, introduced the first meeting. He redelivered the famous lecture on the Everest expedition which many schoolchildren, now grown up, recalled hearing at the Festival Hall in June 1953. Other famous participants were lone yachtsman, Sir Alec Rose, Sir Vivian Fuchs, Laurens van der Post, and Dame Freya Stark.

Westminster Cathedral not normally a bastion of colour, burgeoned into an International Festival of Flowers and Music at the end of June with evening concerts and lunchtime organ recitals. As the Duchess of Norfolk, President of the Festival, had promised, every square inch of that huge edifice was ablaze with flowers. The delicate Japanese art of Ikebana could be seen there, and India sent a florist over specially to arrange Himalayan flowers.

On 23 and 24 July Hyde Park became the arena for the Jubilee Sport For All Spectacular, the national launch of the Sports Council's 1977 'Sport For All' Campaign. Shortly before the weekend, Roger Bottomley of the Sports Council said 'One of the marvellous things about the Jubilee is the way in which everybody has co-operated to make the

Princess Alexandra talking to young sailors at Jubilee Sport for All Spectacular in Hyde Park on 24 July.

Left A view from the helicopter 500 feet above Hyde Park. The Parachutist does not jump until the helicopter is about 2,000 feet above the ground.

Right Free-fall parachuting in Hyde Park.

Below left One of the balloons tethered in Hyde Park.

Below Angus Ogilvy and his son James about to take off in a balloon.

sporting Spectacular possible. It is not every year that we have the opportunity to lay on such a dramatic demonstration of sport in the heart of London. I am confident that many thousands of people will thoroughly enjoy themselves. I also believe that many of these by "having a go" will develop a new interest which could bring them enjoyment and satisfaction for many years to come.'

The Spectacular included the first regatta on the Serpentine for fifteen years with both rowing and canoeing. There was a demonstration of parachuting by members of the Grenadier Guards Free Fall Parachute Team. With their customary skill, they landed within a few feet of the appointed mark each time; a misjudgement could have landed them in Park Lane. Throughout both days there was a continual display of sports, such as volleyball, yoga, croquet and gymnastics. Amateur dancing competitions attracted all ages, with some tiny children, dressed in white ties and ballroom gowns, showing great style and confidence. For those people who prefer something more stirring, there was a display of martial arts which included participants leaping over one another and breaking bricks, and their version of William Tell, in which the apple is dislodged by a quick flick of the left heel. A stern warning was given to those whose proclivities direct them to engage in conversation with young ladies on the benches of Hyde Park. Several examples of the way the young ladies might respond all ended with the man brought to his knees in a couple of brisk manoeuvres.

On Sunday, in addition to these events, there was cycle racing on North Carriage Drive and show jumping in which competitors included Harvey Smith and Captain Mark Phillips. Princess Alexandra, Mr Angus Ogilvy and their son James, toured the events that afternoon, and though weather did not permit a mass balloon ascent, some of them went up tethered and Mr Ogilvy and his son had the chance to 'come up and try it'. Ballooning is a fine example of life's struggle. A powerful injection of air succeeds in getting them off the ground and all seems to be well, but almost immediately further energy is required to prevent them sinking back to ground level. About 4,000 competitors took part in the Spectacular, and the winners went home with gold, silver and bronze medallions presented by the London Celebrations Committee.

Two weeks later the final rounds of the London Jubilee Youth Games took place at Crystal Palace. This was the first ever inter-borough youth games and all thirty-two of them took part with enthusiasm. To be eligible, competitors had to be under twenty-one and resident in a London Borough. The preliminary rounds had taken place at various sporting centres throughout London during the course of the summer, under the auspices of the governing bodies of each sport.

On Saturday, 6 August, all the competitors gathered in the Indoor Arena of the National Sports Centre. Jeffrey Sterling and Jimmy Hill addressed the guests and Mr Sterling read out a message from the Queen, which arrived by relay runners from Buckingham Palace. The

Karate taking place at Crystal Palace in the Jubilee Youth Games on 7 August.

Volleyball in the central stadium of Crystal Palace.

timing was so perfect that certain cynics suggested that the last two runners had had to run on the spot for a few minutes outside the arena to give the impression of having striven valiantly to get there on time.

On the first day, five-a-side association football and netball were played outside, while badminton, fencing, gymnastics, squash, swimming, diving and weight lifting took place indoors. Of these, squash continued on the following day. On Sunday, there were athletics in the stadium, cycling on the circuit, skiing on the special artificial slope, lawn tennis, volleyball and basketball. Each sport engendered its own enthusiasts, who expressed themselves in engaging ways. The spectators of judo urged their man to strangle, squeeze, or otherwise lay waste to his opponent. They returned home, no doubt, with their tensions much relaxed. Karate is a sport of considerable speed. So swift was the action in one round that the losing competitor found himself hurled into the lap of a Mayor of one of the boroughs, seated at the ringside with more enthusiasm for the contest than care for self-preservation.

On Sunday afternoon at 5.30, all the competitors and spectators gathered in the stadium to hear which borough had won on aggregate points. A marching band and some kung-fu dancers entertained the crowd while the scores were added up. Hammersmith came third, Croydon second, and the trophy was presented by Angus Ogilvy to the winning borough Havering. At the end of the day it was hoped that this would be the first of many such Youth Games.

Further extraordinary things happened. Illtyd Harrington, whose instigatory enthusiasm had been curbed somewhat by illness, made a curious discovery in a specially built shelter not a hundred yards from County Hall. This was the Festival of Britain flagpole, which was fashioned from the solid trunk of a Canadian Redwood tree. With due ceremony it was raised to its full 110 feet in the Jubilee Gardens on 28 March. On another occasion Harrington was seen astride the South Bank Lion, brush in hand, giving the back of the lion's ears a scrub to boost a campaign to clean up London's statues.

Sir Paul Wright raising the Jubilee flag at 4 Carlton Gardens in February.

Illtyd Harrington astride the South Bank Lion, boosting a campaign to clean up London's statues.

Part of the Mall decorations and *below* one of the twenty-five silver buses which ran between April and November.

In February Sir Paul Wright risked vertigo and cold winds to raise the Silver Jubilee flag over the Carlton Gardens headquarters of the London Celebrations Committee. The same day the Boroughs raised their Jubilee flags over Town Halls across London and a campaign began to get flags flying and streets decorated on as many buildings as possible. A particularly popular flag was the 'white on red' one which flew from Apsley House and could be seen from all approaches to Hyde Park Corner.

An Easter Parade with a difference hailed the appearance in London of twenty-five silver buses. The buses processed from Hyde Park to Battersea Park and were in service on key Central London routes until November. Embellished with specially fitted carpets, each bus attracted a single sponsor who paid £10,000 for exclusive advertising rights.

The Prince of Wales defined the word Jubilee as 'a cause for jubilation and celebration'. 1977 was certainly a year to be out having fun in whatever way appealed. Apart from the parties, the concerts, the spectaculars and the exhibitions, a lot of people celebrated by putting out decorations, a travel firm made a 'one day only' offer of holidays at 1952 prices and Mary Wilson wrote a poem. Besides all the things that did happen, there were numerous events of course that were planned but did not take place. Early Jubilee press-cuttings are full of councillors who have spark but not fire, men who get publicity by announcing stupendous plans but have not the stamina to see them through.

At previous Jubilees, generous pardons had been granted to certain wrong-doers. George III, for example, sanctioned an amnesty for some military and naval prisoners. He also extended the pardon to some deserters, and released prisoners of war (but not Frenchmen apparently). Penny Symon, who covered the Jubilee for *The Times*, suggested dispensations suitable for 1977, including 'an amnesty on overdue library books' and 'a moratorium on parking fines'. Alas, these were not granted.

What's Left?

At the end of the year when the flags are lowered and once shining decorations, now a little tired, are peeled off the side of buildings, what is left?

Celebrations are by their nature ephemeral, but, if enjoyed, remain forever as a happy memory. Henry James wrote that there are disappointments which last as long as life; conversely these happy memories cannot be taken away however dark life may become. To spend £50,000 on a firework display which lasted thirty minutes might well seem extravagant but a firework display is just as vivid as one walk in a new garden to someone who never returns there. The displays were watched free by many millions of people, either gathered in London or in the comfort of their own homes. ABC, the American network discovered that the coverage of bonfire night and the procession to St. Paul's had gained higher audience ratings than their own Bicentennial the year before. Thus they also filmed the fireworks which were seen in the United States, and gripped the imagination of the Americans, who were beginning to think the British were no longer capable of such things. Children in the States were even allowed off school to watch the broadcasts.

The largest single environmental project in 1977 was the construction of the Jubilee Gardens on the old Festival of Britain site between the County Hall and Festival Hall. Work progressed at tremendous speed and the gardens were completed in good time for their official opening by the Queen. In May Lord Drogheda presented a scroll to the then Chairman of the GLC, Lord Ponsonby of Shulbrede on the completion of the work. The scroll told something of the history of the site. 'In the course of its varied history it has been occupied by a stone manufactory, a brewery, a glassworks, a warehouse, an helicopter pad and latterly a car park'. The cost of the gardens was estimated at £300,000. During a brief spell of hot weather Londoners found their way there and as Noel Coward put it 'assumed a horizontal status and relaxed'. On 21 July a Beano was held in aid of Action Research for the Crippled

St Paul's Cathedral and *above* Buckingham Palace, floodlit.

A three-dimensional symbol in Leicester Square, marking the start of the Silver Jubilee Walkway.

Child; a discotheque played, fireworks were let off, and bumper cars and roundabouts were in full swing. Floodlighting played on nearby buildings and attracted many passers-by. Also in July part of the City Music Trail Concerts were heard there.

In August 1975 Max Nicholson saw the Jubilee as an opportunity to create some lasting good throughout London. In this he correctly interpreted popular feeling that out of the festivities should come something solid for the general enjoyment in years to come. He produced a document called 'The Seven Thrusts' in which he declared he was not content to leave 'a haphazard legacy of scattered unrelated Jubilee halls, gardens, fountains, seats and suchlike' but intended to initiate an overall plan for ongoing projects in partnership with local authorities and voluntary bodies.

The first two thrusts aimed to knit London more closely together. The Silver Jubilee Walkway was one way of doing this. Starting from Leicester Square the walker passes through Trafalgar Square, St. James's Park and Parliament Square. He continues through Victoria Tower Gardens, where he can inspect the progress of the Queen's Lucombe Oak. Then he crosses Lambeth Bridge to the South Bank, following the Thames closely all the way to Tower Bridge, which he crosses and arrives at Tower Hill, having completed five and a quarter miles. The Walkway is marked by a series of London Celebrations paving stones, which, when they first appeared, confused and fascinated Londoners. In the course of his walk, the pedestrian will have travelled through areas of the city noted for entertainment, assembly, ceremonial, open-air activities and national history. He will have been enticed from the West End onto the South Bank and into the City. Max Nicholson hinted that perhaps he will be subtly changed by what he has absorbed from 'this fertile heritage'.

Left The Jubilee Gardens on the Southbank after and before landscaping

The Silver Jubilee Walkway map.

Further along the route, close to HMS *Belfast*, lies the Ecological Park, another of 1977's projects. This was three acres of derelict land which is being turned into an area of woodland, grassland and fresh-water pools. It is the first serious attempt in London to recreate closer links with nature.

The second thrust was to knit North London together by the fuller use of the Regent's Canal and the Grand Union Canal. By opening the towpath it will eventually be possible, given the necessary stamina and some stout walking shoes, to perambulate along a car-free route from the Colne Valley to the Lea Valley, a distance of some twenty miles.

The third thrust was directed at Covent Garden. St. Paul's Church famed for its architecture and its associations with the world of thespians, opera singers and ballet dancers, had its portico cleaned and its garden reorganised. On the site of the old Tin Market, the Italian Garden, designed to harmonise with Inigo Jones's original concept of the Piazza with St. Paul's Church at one end and the Opera House at the

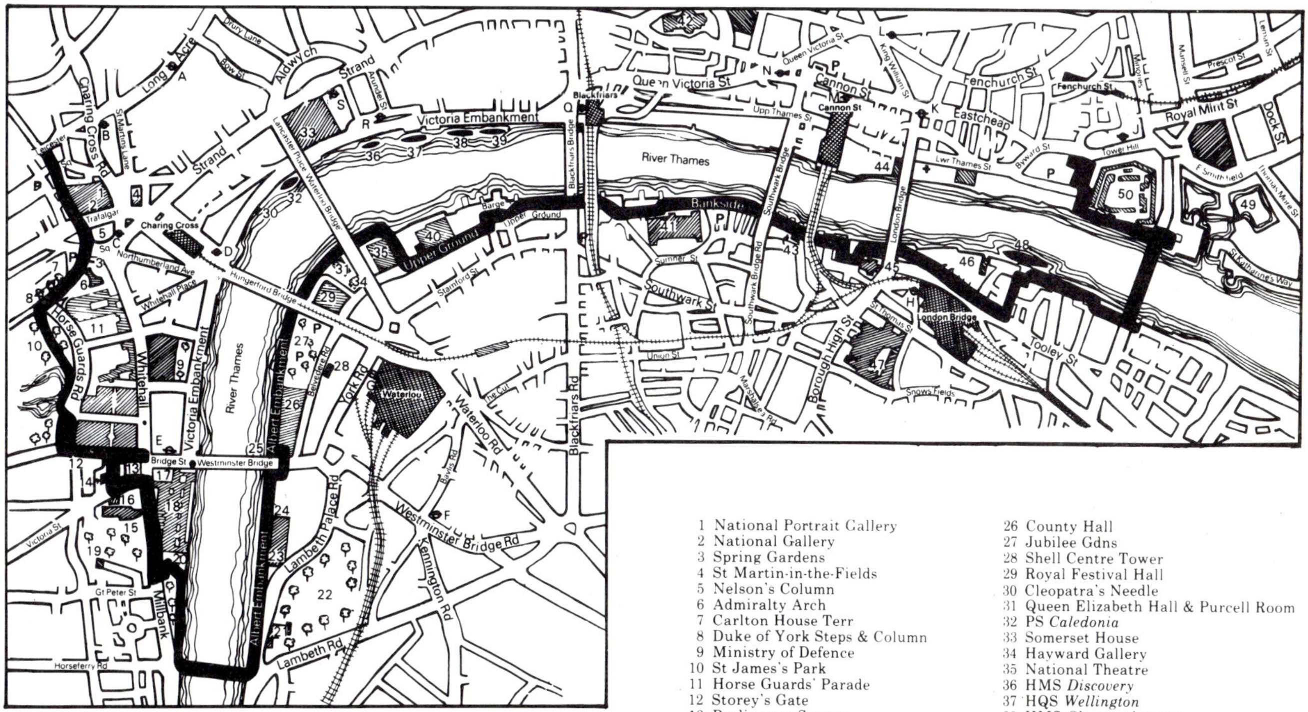

1 National Portrait Gallery	14 Guildhall	26 County Hall	39 HMS *President*
2 National Gallery	15 Westminster Abbey	27 Jubilee Gdns	40 South Bank TV Centre
3 Spring Gardens	16 St Margaret's Church	28 Shell Centre Tower	41 Bankside Power Station
4 St Martin-in-the-Fields	17 Westminster Hall	29 Royal Festival Hall	42 St Paul's Cathedral
5 Nelson's Column	18 Houses of Parliament	30 Cleopatra's Needle	43 Anchor pub
6 Admiralty Arch	19 Jewel Tower	31 Queen Elizabeth Hall & Purcell Room	44 Fishmongers Hall
7 Carlton House Terr	20 Victoria Tower Gdns	32 PS *Caledonia*	45 Southwark Cathedral
8 Duke of York Steps & Column	21 Lambeth Palace	33 Somerset House	46 Hay's Wharf
9 Ministry of Defence	22 Lambeth Palace Gdns	34 Hayward Gallery	47 Guys Hospital
10 St James's Park	23 St Thomas's Medical School	35 National Theatre	48 HMS *Belfast*
11 Horse Guards' Parade	24 St Thomas's Hospital	36 HMS *Discovery*	49 St Katherine Yacht Haven
12 Storey's Gate	25 South Bank Lion	37 HQS *Wellington*	50 Tower of London
13 Parliament Square		38 HMS *Chrysanthemum*	

Underground Stations

A Covent Garden
B Leicester Sq
C Trafalgar Sq
D Embankment
E Westminster
F Lambeth North
G Waterloo
H London Bridge
J Tower Hill
K Monument
L Bank
M Cannon St
N Mansion House
Q Blackfriars
R Temple
S Aldwych

Walkway

P Car Parks

other, was opened by the Duke of Gloucester at the end of September. In addition to this a Small Enterprise Centre was opened on 6 July at the Warehouse Gallery, Earlham Street. Its aim is to foster collaboration amongst small enterprise. The Centre hopes to take over and develop some of the decaying empty spaces, such as disused warehouses, which are becoming so much a part of urban life.

Thrust number four was a London-wide heritage and amenity programme through the Civic Trust. Greater London has 99 local amenity societies and each one was invited to suggest improvement schemes to mark the Silver Jubilee. Five factors were taken into account when plans were made. The schemes should be finished by the end of 1977, they should be of lasting value, they should aim for the maximum return for the minimum outlay of funds, they should challenge problems previously thought of as insuperable (for example a site that had lain derelict for years) and they should attempt some background projects such as providing guidance notes for those who live in a conservation area. Thirty-nine amenity societies suggested 71 schemes between them. Of these 46 were granted funds in 25 out of the 32 boroughs. The schemes were often highly imaginative and varied from the restoration of a 17th century milestone to the creation of an adventure playground on derelict land.

The Queen planted the first tree in the tree-planting programme, which was the fifth thrust. All parts of Greater London were urged to

Drums being made at the Small Enterprise Centre in Earl Street.

Meanwhile Gardens, Paddington before and after.

Opposite Princess Anne with some of the schoolchildren who greeted her when she opened Newham City Farm on 19 July.

plant and maintain trees, so many of which had been lost either through Dutch Elm Disease or recent development.

London had 40,000 acres of land lying idle and derelict, some of it seemingly deserted forever and other parts waiting for some project delayed by inertia or lack of funds. The sixth thrust singled out six different sites to show what could be done and open the way for further improvements in the future. The Meanwhile Gardens occupied a three and a half-acre open space bordering the canal in Elkstone Road, Paddington. It had been derelict for at least ten years. The plan to turn it into a community garden was an ambitious one. A Job Creation Team of fourteen created a bicycling scrambling track, Britain's first ever skateboard track, an open air theatre for plays and concerts, and a quiet garden where old people could sit in peace amongst roses and vegetables observing the young playing and yet protected from the general action. Chicken and rabbits can be housed there, workshops have been constructed to encourage local crafts and the Grand Union Canal can be used for boating. On a random visit in the summer the garden was full of citizens of all ages, a pop-group was playing and children were climbing a wall and competing on the track.

The Mudchute was a rubbish-strewn area, which had once been the tip for mud excavated when Millwall Docks were dug. The plan was to retain the wild character of the area but to put down a network of paths and plants. Originally a formal garden was planned, but this was vandalised and thus disbanded. However, an urban city farm has been built there and is being very successful.

Newham City Farm is another urban city farm, built on some unused land at Becton, which had once been playing fields. The Mayflower Family Centre ran the project, which was worked on by eight adults and sixteen young people provided by the Manpower Services Commission. By the time that Princess Anne opened the farm on 19 July, the farm boasted four horses, eight goats, two cows, ten ducks, seventy chickens, eight bantams, a guinea pig and some sixty rabbits (no doubt a rapidly multiplying figure). Princess Anne, on one of her last public engagements before having her baby, was greeted by over 1,000 local schoolchildren and presented not only with flowers but with some eggs and a bottle of elderflower champagne from the farm.

The Duke of Gloucester opened another site underneath the arches of Westway on 12 July. Portobello Green described as 'recently the haunt of alcoholics and vandals in the centre of an area of racial tension' became a small park with a sheltered play area and a bonfire site. At the same time, Emily Young, a young London artist, painted a series of brightly coloured murals on the arches of Westway. The Duke had visited the site earlier in the year when it was still a mudbath, and so was able to see the transformation for himself.

Finally, the Clerkenwell Trust for Urban Development was established to undertake improvements in the Clerkenwell urban areas and

Opposite The Duke of Gloucester underneath the arches of Westway with Emily Young, who painted the murals, at the opening of Portobello Green on 12 July.

to make sure that derelict sites and buildings did not remain unused.

The seventh thrust was the *Clean Up London Campaign*. Its aims were to encourage residents and tourists to keep the streets clean, to reduce the length of time when bins and refuse were left on the pavements awaiting collection, to encourage building owners to clean dirty buildings, and to attack London's eyesores. In other words it was a plan to give London a facelift for Jubilee year and do everything possible to ensure that work continued. Amongst buildings cleaned were St. Paul's Church, Covent Garden, the Grand Buildings in Trafalgar Square, and the west front of St. Mary-le-Strand. In July anti-litter pilot schemes were organised in two black spots, Wembley and Hyde Park, where Jubilee events were taking place. Splendid posters were issued showing a Pearly Queen with industrious citizens in the background and the message 'Keep our street clean fit for a Queen'. A clean-up float was planned to take part in the Lord Mayor of London's show in November. The floor of St. Paul's Cathedral was given a one day clean to demonstrate modern methods of cleaning. Earlier in the year the Pearly Kings and Queens of London toured most of the boroughs in their specially decorated buses. They presented Mayors and senior council officers with colourful brooms and set them straight to work.

Lord Drogheda was keen that London should be widely floodlit in 1977. This was greeted with the opinion that since the fuel crisis was only three years ago it would not be a propitious time. Lord Drogheda was adamant, however, 'What more propitious time could there be than the Queen's Jubilee?' he asked. Tom Masterson set to work. In September 1976 the *Electrical Review* published some statistics which aided the Light Up London Campaign. Apsley House was cited as an example. Evidently, in connexion with European Architectural Heritage Year 1975, a splendid floodlighting installation had been put in, but had been switched on on only one occasion. The Director of a large electrical company noted that the cost of lighting Apsley House was a trivial 11.5p an hour. Thus if it was lit for an average 600 hours a year, the total cost would be £196, about the sum that an average overseas tourist would spend during a stay in the capital. Apsley House was one of many buildings lit during the summer. Buckingham Palace and the Mall, and the many buildings along the Thames were specially lit. Some tall buildings reversed the process and picked out E II R in the lights of their offices for a time. Both the Clean Up and the Light Up London campaigns will continue in future years.

London Looks Forward was a major study conference on the future of London which took place on 4 and 5 July at the Queen Elizabeth Hall. Following the Duke of Edinburgh's two Countryside Conferences in the sixties, which were hailed as 'a turning point in the history of conservation' in this country, the *London Looks Forward* conference looked objectively at the economic and social aspects of London's major problems. Before the conference, Thames Television set out to

HONOURABLE EQUITY LONDON PEARLY
Let it Be a litter free Jubilee in Brent
Keep Britain Tidy
Let it Be a litter free Jubilee in Brent
Keep Britain Tidy

Left Four Pearly Kings and Queens showing how it's done with brooms they gave Mayors at Wembley.

Some of the ladies who help keep London clean with the Dean of St Paul's outside the Cathedral.

involve as many people as possible in expressing their views, by special television programmes, interviews and debates in the press. Ten *London Looks Forward* programmes went out each Friday on the 'Today' programme at 6.00 pm., and Thames devoted peak viewing time to a special programme before and after 'News at Ten' on 22 June. A competition was run to encourage schools to contribute their ideas in connexion with the schools programme *London – The Making of a City*. Transportation, housing, employment and environmental improvements were deliberated with a view to enhancing the quantity of life in London. The Duke of Edinburgh took part, being a seasoned conference man, and he also appeared in a second special television programme after the conference was over.

When the main Jubilee events were over, Lord Drogheda received a letter from Merlyn Rees, the Home Secretary, thanking him and the London Celebrations Committee for 'all you have done to make this such a memorable occasion for Londoners'. The Home Secretary con-

The Royal Family modelled in Jubilee year as they were in 1952 by Madame Tussaud's, London.

tinued 'From the major events like the firework displays (which I was fortunate enough to attend and enjoyed a great deal) and the Covent Garden Gala, to the street parties and local entertainments, your Committee's activities have ensured that all Londoners have had the opportunity to celebrate the occasion in the proper style. And we can all be specially grateful for the permanent additions to London's amenities which have been brought about by the work of your Environmental Committee providing a series of lasting memorials to the Jubilee'.

'We want the Queen'.